Soils

by Grace Hansen

Abdo
GEOLOGY ROCKS!
Kids

abdopublishing.com

Published by Abdo Kids, a division of ABDO, PO Box 398166, Minneapolis, Minnesota 55439.

Copyright © 2016 by Abdo Consulting Group, Inc. International copyrights reserved in all countries. No part of this book may be reproduced in any form without written permission from the publisher.

Printed in the United States of America, North Mankato, Minnesota.

052015

092015

Photo Credits: iStock, Shutterstock

Production Contributors: Teddy Borth, Jennie Forsberg, Grace Hansen

Design Contributors: Laura Rask, Dorothy Toth

Library of Congress Control Number: 2014958429

Cataloging-in-Publication Data

Hansen, Grace.

 Soils / Grace Hansen.

  p. cm. -- (Geology rocks!)

ISBN 978-1-62970-910-9

Includes index.

1. Soils--Juvenile literature.   I. Title.

577--dc23

            2014958429

Table of Contents

Soil 4

Soil is Alive 10

Loam 16

Soil Gives Life 20

Main Ingredients of Soil 22

Glossary 23

Index 24

Abdo Kids Code 24

Soil

Soil is the top layer
of Earth's surface. Soil
is almost everywhere.

Soil comes in many colors.

It can be black or brown.

It can be red or white.

7

Crushed rock is found in soil.

Air and water are in soil, too.

Soil is Alive

Many tiny living things are in soil. They are called **microbes**.

microbes

Microbes are very small.

Most are too small to see.

But they have big jobs to do.

Bacteria and fungi are **microbes**. They break down dead plants and animals. This gives soil lots of **nutrients**.

15

Loam

The best soil for growing

plants is dark. It is soft.

It crumbles in your hands.

This soil is called loam.

Loam is a mix of sand and **silt**. There is also a little bit of **clay** in it.

Soil Gives Life

Soil is **necessary** for life on Earth. Plants could not grow without soil. Humans and animals eat plants.

20

Main Ingredients of Soil

organic matter

water

air

minerals

22

Glossary

clay – a heavy, sticky material, from the earth that is made mostly of fine particles and minerals. It is used for brick, tile, and pottery.

microbes – very small living things that can only be seen with a microscope.

necessary – so important that it must happen.

nutrients – substances that plants, animals, and people need to live and grow.

organic matter – matter that occurs naturally. It can be alive or dead. Includes leaves, dead plants, microbes, etc.

silt – very small particles that are smaller than sand, but larger than clay.

Index

animals 14, 20

color 6

contents 8, 10, 14

humans 20

loam 16, 18

microbes 10, 12, 14

nutrients 14

plants 14, 20

abdokids.com

Use this code to log on to abdokids.com and access crafts, games, videos, and more!

Abdo Kids Code:
GSK9109